"*Full Worm Moon* calls to mind both the cycle of monthly full moons that structures this collection, and the change that arrives in the loosening of the earth at the end of winter. But change and hope are two different things. As one poem puts it: 'Sometimes there's no such thing/as a fresh start.' And yet Moore knows, as the first section of poems chart her marital breakup and the way broken vows rend one's sense of the sacred, that while the world around her cannot take her pain away, it can help absorb it. And so, as this cycle of poems turns ever outward—to family, friends, paintings, books, and the natural world—Moore slowly rights herself, allowing the beauty that comes our way without our asking to do what it does best: bring the grace of new possibilities. There is a casual mastery in these poems—Moore's attention to details allows the most ordinary of moments to tip, without the slightest poetic willfulness, into the extraordinary. And, equally tuned to life's harshness and life's beneficence, Moore's *Full Worm Moon* finds a way to bless 'this place [we] wander through' even as life's sorrows are endured."

–Robert Cording
author of *Only So Far*

"In a lyric voice infused with Julie L. Moore's own enduring faith, this collection mines the ruins of a longtime marriage and a woman's solo journey towards restoration. These marvelous poems return to the locus of changing seasons, marital strife, and love—in the darkness of the fallibly human overturned by the eternal brightness of the divine. . . Here is a remarkable book, in all its graceful beauty and savagery, to savor one syllable at a time: 'Dusk lifts the light from view/I know this first-hand/then hides it like a key beneath a stone.'"

–Karen An-hwei Lee
author of *Phyla of Joy*

"The full moon rises each month throughout this moving collection, shining down on 'the gritty corridors/of [a] long marriage,' as we watch it painfully unravel... Moore knows how to pay attention, following Simone Weil's dictum, "absolutely unmixed attention is prayer," showing us minute details like the "dusk's mauve gauze / drap[ing] around our shoulders." Because the book ends with 'as you take each successive step,' we know that she's safe on her journey, a path she didn't choose, a woman newly and bravely alone. Beautifully crafted and artfully wrought, these poems will sear themselves on your memory long after you close the book."

–Barbara Crooker
author of *Les Fauves*

"'What if the beautiful day is over?' wonders Julie Moore in her shattering new collection, *Full Worm Moon*. And indeed, poems about the end of a marriage wring the reader...These poems are rich with empathy for all living creatures, especially the exploited and abused. It's not hard to imagine Jesus striding through the cow pastures and Little League stadiums of Moore's poems. Amidst the world's disarray, Moore's playful wit and exultant language ultimately proclaim the persistence of tenderness, peace, and love."

–Anna Krugovoy Silver
author of *Second Bloom* and *From Nothing*

Full Worm Moon

The Poiema Poetry Series

Poems are windows into worlds; windows into beauty, goodness, and truth; windows into understandings that won't twist themselves into tidy dogmatic statements; windows into experiences. We can do more than merely peer into such windows; with a little effort we can fling open the casements, and leap over the sills into the heart of these worlds. We are also led into familiar places of hurt, confusion, and disappointment, but we arrive in the poet's company. Poetry is a partnership between poet and reader, seeking together to gain something of value—to get at something important.

Ephesians 2:10 says, "We are God's workmanship..." *poiema* in Greek—the thing that has been made, the masterpiece, the poem. The Poiema Poetry Series presents the work of gifted poets who take Christian faith seriously, and demonstrate in whose image we have been made through their creativity and craftsmanship.

These poets are recent participants in the ancient tradition of David, Asaph, Isaiah, and John the Revelator. The thread can be followed through the centuries—through the diverse poetic visions of Dante, Bernard of Clairvaux, Donne, Herbert, Milton, Hopkins, Eliot, R. S. Thomas, and Denise Levertov—down to the poet whose work is in your hand. With the selection of this volume you are entering this enduring tradition, and as a reader contributing to it.

—D.S. Martin
Series Editor

Full Worm Moon

A Book of Poems

by
JULIE L. MOORE

CASCADE *Books* • Eugene, Oregon

FULL WORM MOON
A Book of Poems

The Poiema Poetry Series

Copyright © 2018 Julie L. Moore. All rights reserved. Except for brief quotations in critical publications or reviews, no part of this book may be reproduced in any manner without prior written permission from the publisher. Write: Permissions, Wipf and Stock Publishers, 199 W. 8th Ave., Suite 3, Eugene, OR 97401.

Cascade Books
An Imprint of Wipf and Stock Publishers
199 W. 8th Ave., Suite 3
Eugene, OR 97401

www.wipfandstock.com

PAPERBACK ISBN: 978-1-5326-4760-4
HARDCOVER ISBN: 978-1-5326-4761-1
EBOOK ISBN: 978-1-5326-4762-8

Cataloguing-in-Publication data:

Names: Moore, Julie L., author.
Title: Full worm moon : a book of poems / Julie L. Moore.
Description: Eugene, OR: Cascade Books, 2018. | The Poiema Poetry Series.
Identifiers: ISBN 978-1-5326-4760-4 (paperback). | ISBN 978-1-5326-4761-1 (hardcover). | ISBN 978-1-5326-4762-8 (epub).
Subjects: LCSH: American poetry—21st century.
Classification: PS3563.O6215 F27 2018 (print). | PS3563.O6215 (epub).

Manufactured in the U.S.A.   03/08/18

To Ashley, Alex, & Abi

Adonai's best gifts

Contents

FULL THUNDER MOON

Loose Stone, | 3
Full Wolf Moon | 4
Nocturne | 5
Full Hunger Moon | 7
Tear | 8
Clear Water | 10
Baseball | 12
The Ring | 13
Bow Echo | 14
Four days after Mother's Day, | 15
Nightmare | 17
Compline | 19
Full Thunder Moon | 20
Weights & Measures | 22
I never met a flower that yelled at me, | 23
Barley Moon | 25
PTSD | 27
Once, | 28
In a parallel universe, | 30
Full Long Nights Moon | 31

AFTERSHOCK

Full Worm Moon | 35
Mailbox | 36
Palm Sunday | 38
Aftershock | 40
Comet | 42
I was led to believe | 44

Where were you when you realized | 46
Strawberry Moon | 47
No Heaven | 49
Barn Burning | 53
Reflex | 54
Orb Weaver | 55
Cooper's Hawks | 56
Coming Close | 58
Following the Light | 59
Walking on the Roof | 61
Milton | 63
Morning Prayer | 64
Blackberry Seeds | 65
There Is No Violence Here | 67
Moon When Horns Are Broken Off | 68
Easy Prey | 69
Close Range | 71
Present | 72
The Road My Daughter Drives On | 73
Nest in a Winter Tree | 75
Molasses | 76
In Which the Magpie Resurrects the Voice of Henry David Thoreau | 78

THIS IS THE LANDSCAPE LEFT

Objects in Mirror Are Closer Than They Appear | 81
Ode to a Pumpkin Patch Discovered By a Trail | 82
Hope | 84
Science Lesson | 85
The Philosopher & the Poet Talk on the Last Warm Day in Fall | 87
The Problem with School | 88
Piano Lesson | 89
Lament | 91
Certainty | 93
Cryoseism | 94
What If Feels Like, | 95
The Conversation of Wood | 96
Blood Moon | 97
This is the landscape left | 98

What the Stone Knows | 100
Vessels | 102
Sparrow | 104
Full Flower Moon | 105
Open Window One Summer Night | 107
Hesperis Matronalis | 108
Big Basin Sagebrush | 110
Yellow Springs, Ohio | 111
The Poet Performs in the Theatre of Cows | 112
Heartland | 114
Moon When All Things Ripen | 116
Serpent Mound | 118
Three Questions | 120

Acknowledgments | 123
Awards & Recognitions | 126

Full Thunder Moon

Loose Stone,

      the orange sign reads, as she turns
onto her country road, heading home
      where empty rooms will greet her,
left behind as her husband & she are
      since the kids cleared out for college.

This is far from upheaval,
      yet everything feels disturbed,
treacherous as this fresh macadam
      when too much speed meets
the sharp curve ahead.

Yesterday, their dog stood
      at the top of the stairs, whining,
restoring noise to the floors.
      She almost let the Lab go on,
savoring the company

of her misery, acute & close,
      though her dark pitch
fused with fears loosed
      down the gritty corridors
of their long marriage.

Full Wolf Moon

The pink tulip from the store
droops, bowing its heavy head
below the vase's rim, the face

of the full wolf moon beaming
through the window, illuminating
the collapse within,

the husband confessing to his wife
he told another woman she was
beautiful,

exhuming the wife's memory
of Jimmy Lynch in middle school,
the two of them alone, hall passes in hand,

heading in opposite directions,
when he eyed her, then growled,
You are such a dog.

His comment a paw in a fertile field
digging at roots that try hard
to hold fast, roots the husband now

wrenches free & tosses aside
in the same darkness where wolves howl,
syncopating their guts' insistent pangs

to the beat of the sacred vow's heart.

Nocturne

Sight does no good here.
Whether on her back, or on her face,
she can't see what is happening.

She can only hear something
like an owl, or its prey, crying
in the wee hours of the morning.

It's so dark, I can't see my hand,
she thinks to herself as she lies in bed
beside the man who said

nothing to her this evening
when she asked, for the first time ever,
Are you going to leave me?

He speaks now, though, moaning,
Help me! Get off of me! Help!
She waits a minute, lets him struggle,

then rubs his shoulder, tells him to wake.
He mumbles his sleep's terrifying story:
Tied down with ropes, surrounded by phantoms

who hovered over him, even pressed
against his chest, he could not break free.
Falling back to sleep, his breath quickly

grows heavy. She stays awake all night,
listening to his words reverberate,
their cymbals clashing in the eaves.

Full Hunger Moon

It's February & sludge permeates the snow
that has lain here for a month.

Affection has dimmed to shadow,
her attention cast from what was

to what is, the way entropy changes everything,
the chaos of molecules reverberating—

ice, liquid, dust—as they attempt equilibrium
but leave everything in disarray.

She can't remember what her husband's love felt like.
She can't remember his first touch—his hand reaching

for hers as they walked around the lake.
She can't remember what once was easy,

like rest in the Lord they'd both believed in,
like the snow that showered down in January,

christening the new year with all the possible blessings
beauty brings. Sometimes, there's no such thing

as a fresh start. Sometimes, what falls
gets trapped in the mire & never rises again.

Tear

–with two lines from Gregory Orr

It's Palm Sunday, the day he tells
his wife he doesn't love her anymore,
that the last few years, he's been struggling.

When she asks him about the woman he claims
is just a friend, his eyes shine like silver coins,
his wide smile renounces his tongue.

His wife has *such a longing*
to become the beloved, his beloved,
a longing sharp as a saw & as jagged,

a saw that a Roman may have used
to prepare *crux simplex, crux commissa*,
or *crux immissa*, the pole, the T-shaped gibbet,

the cross itself. He's placed her every flaw
on her head like unforgiving thorns
that press & pierce

as their name becomes legion.
She envisions the people spreading their palms
onto the dusty road, Christ on his donkey

riding forward, longing for them to love him
for who he was, not for who they wished him to be.
She understands she's not holy like he is—she can save

no one—but as she hears him weeping for Jerusalem,
she weeps, too, for she knows how rejoicing
turns to sorrow, how a vow once sincere & right

can ripen beyond its glory, letting in the thing
that slinks between the solemn words
& the lips that formed them,

how everything then leads to rupture—
once the tear begins,
even the holiest of veils rends.

Clear Water

They walk their Lab on McMillan Road,
                the limbs of their lengthy marriage pulled
       from every joint,
           every step, a monumental mission.

Even the dog seems to sense something's wrong,
                as she stays close, letting the leash
       lag. The husband pauses long,
           trying to think of something positive to say,

practice in praise their counselor has advised,
                when a brown figure startles them with its
       sudden forward motion,
           then dives into the nearby stream.

As they approach the creek,
                they see the beaver
       beneath the surface,
           gliding with such ease

no noise, no aftermath
                of turbulence, no wake follows—
       if the water
           weren't clear, they'd never know the animal was there.

Maybe they'd all like to jump in—
                the dog for the glory of the swim,
       the husband
           for the hope of cleansing,

the wife for the progress of her body
                    toward something else,
           away from this road
                 they've all been treading.

Baseball

As they watch the Indians,
she hopes their common interest, which inspired

their mutual friend to unite them 28 years ago,
will ignite a comeback, rally his will

to renew the love he says has diminished to nothing.
They watch the Tigers pile on runs

while she thumbs through the paper & he plays
the game of checking scores online.

Though he tries to keep his signs secret,
she catches him stealing electric

glances with another woman.
The field isn't even. She can sense

loss prevailing, its steel cleats rounding
third, heading for home.

The Ring

One day, the husband removes his ring,
tossing it in his jewelry box
with pennies, tie clips, & slips
of paper, then heads to work
where he pledges his allegiance.
There, the other woman has eclipsed his wife.
There, he lives in another universe.
Here, his bare finger intercepts light
as his hand wraps around a glass of Coke,
& his wife perceives the problem
darkening what hope
was left beneath her sternum.
This is an alien realm, her new home
a sphere of confusion, of love overthrown.

Bow Echo

Their ornamental pear tree,
    like her once-whole heart,
        broke in this morning's storm:

        Manic & maniacal, the wind's crow-
    bar pried limbs from the trunk,
peeled off bark, exposing everything.

Across the street, the birch tree
    is uprooted, prostrate on the ground
        like one spouse pleading

    with the other not to leave.
    The weatherman says a bow echo's
dying line toppled these trees,

companions once constant & true,
    as they faced one another every day,
        sharing air from another life.

Four days after Mother's Day,

her husband enters the house, & again, her body shakes,
first her stomach, quivering in its acid,
then her back & shoulders tightening,
curling her, not into a ball,
but into a hunchback, a grotesque formed
by fear, for he is here—

he who threatened over & over to leave her,
even on Mother's Day as she lay in bed,
nausea festering in her throat like streptococcus,
gagging her, driving her under sheet & quilt,
where she prayed like King David, *Do not be far
from me, for trouble is near*,

& begged for her bones to stop burning.
He loomed over her, not to give her
flowers & offer his deepest apology,
but to hand her a card that read, *What a gift you are*,
then warning, again, *If you won't let me
be friends with her*,

I'm leaving you.
Today, she hovers over pots of sauce & pasta,
water in one, trembling like her hands,
then boiling over before her eyes,
scalding the stove top's ceramic skin,
ominous aura

of sizzle & smoke blinding
her every breath. *I love you*, he'd said
to his daughter, home from college that terrible May day
when he did what he promised & left—then came back.
I wish you loved my mom, she'd countered
(wanting to untie

the knot of his manipulation,
expose the divided heart at the center
of his universe), daughter who now sits at the table
while marinara splatters
democratically—
                          here, here, & here.

Nightmare

Just weeks before their wedding, she dreamed
she screamed at him for no apparent reason,
then stabbed him as his hands veiled his face.
When she awoke, she was relieved to be lying
in her bed & dismissed the nightmare, blaming
its origin on (what else?) her period.
But two nights later, her sleep blossomed
into the same reddish vision. Once conscious,
she thought twice, she really did.
She started wondering about signs.
Twenty-six years later, she is slapping
his arm, then the small of his back,
overcome by the cut of his serrated
words, mocking her because she snores,
threatening to leave her for another woman,
packing clothes & toiletries every morning,
saying he might not return.
She apologizes as soon as her hand
lifts from his skin, begs
for his forgiveness, weeps like the penitent
sinner she is. He leaves.
(He will always hold close the skeleton
of her body's work, raise each bone like a spear).
She sees their counselor, confesses.
She wants to hit herself, slice her wrists.
The counselor says she must not be *so desperate
for her husband's love*. She must *let him go*.
Alone, then, the wife stands in her kitchen,
looking at the beefsteak tomatoes

her mother has given her, a dozen plump & juicy
globes ready to yield bruschetta or salsa
the husband would not thank her for,
would not relish as either drips
down his chin, won't even be around to eat them.
She doesn't know how to begin.

Compline

St. Meinrad Archabbey

Forgive me my faults, my faults, my grievous faults,
she recites with the Benedictines preparing
for evening's darkening shroud—

her husband's figure standing erect
in her memory, his finger pointing at her,
threatening her, his once-sure vows

now dead, their hazy specters
prowling the hallways of her heart,
their long fingernails raking its walls.

While she chants—words, just words,
& barely sung—the Lord's Prayer
stumbles onto her tongue: *forgive us our trespasses,*

as we forgive those who trespass against us.
Not even an hour, nor is it sweet,
this prayer that arrests her,

exorcising the ghosts of promises past,
their furious, furious haunting.

Full Thunder Moon

Be merciful to me, O God, be merciful, for I have taken refuge in you; in the shadow of your wings will I take refuge until this time of trouble has gone by.

–Psalm 57:1

Sitting in the gazebo at St. Meinrad Archabbey,
    she hears the sky grumbling as one cloud swells,
        its lining stretched so thin,
            all she can see is the darkness within.

Dusk slinks in beneath it.
    The first few fireflies flicker.
        Lights go on in each eventual window
            as the monks ready for their simple beds.

At compline, their prayers prepared them for the keening
    that comes with loss, whether of light or life.
        Swatting the occasional mosquito here beneath
            the full thunder moon, she inhales air thick with solace,

the only breath possible with rain pending.
    As the first drops finally fall, she realizes how indifferent they are
        to whether her marriage lasted two years or twenty-seven.
            It's all the same to them as they hurry down

their flights of stairs, every one of them determined
    to skip the last two steps, land hard,
        it doesn't matter where. They are not picky.
            They have no scruples.

So of course, they alight on the bare arms
    of a wife who's endured seven surgeries,
        whose husband left her, then told her,
            Your health problems have worn me out.

This storm doesn't give a rip.
    It doesn't even know it could be used for good,
        showering fields overflowing with barley
            & wheat & corn, as everyone knows,

or driving a woman to seek refuge
    in a place so vulnerable & open,
        a bird, say, a sparrow or finch, might glide in
            & roost right there, within an inch of her care.

Weights & Measures

In the unpredictable calculus of their separation, he comes
    & goes—she can't stop his returning to pour salt

into the softener or trim trees, as though such acts count
    as some sort of penance. He owns the house, too.

So he makes himself at home, sitting at the breakfast bar,
    running through receipts to throw his weights

& measures around, balancing his self-made
    scales of justice in the budget.

The wife washes the dishes, her teeth
    grinding, digging into her tongue,

as her husband subtracts every part of her he can,
    complaining as he goes how inadequate

everything is, how nothing adds up.
    She deciphers how to breathe only when he leaves.

I never met a flower that yelled at me,

her neighbor always says, explaining why,
every year, he plants & hangs
geraniums, begonias, impatiens, petunias,
even blue lobelia, amid his blooming bulbs.

She wants that sentiment to infect her, too,
the summer her husband leaves.
So on the hottest day Ohio can muster, she faces
the roses her husband sunk in soil ten years before.

On the side of the house, they grow weed-loud.
Even cantankerous saplings push through
the bushes, silencing all the kind words in their red mouths.
Everything has to go.

As she digs, thorns & muscular weeds
thick with prickles recite
her husband's remarks on her skin,
scratching, clawing, tearing:

I can't commit to you 100%, only 75%.
Shovel meets hard earth again & again.
Gasping for air, feeling her back spasm in protest,
she clings to the wood handle. *You're too hardline.*

You want too much. She lets the sun scold her,
lets the heavy air weigh on her shoulders,
lets all of it, the whole fucking force
of his question, *What do you mean I disregard you?,*

fuel her resistance, her freedom to say,
No, you & your furious mess
will not stand, not here, not any longer.
In their place, she leaves behind

what perennial peace she can—
pink Asiatic lilies, purple coneflowers,
& threadleaf coreopsis shining
their favor without ridicule or question.

Barley Moon

As she walks her dog,
the sun crouches
like the cat near ripe corn,
which her Lab lunges toward,
yanking her out of loss's all-
consuming reverie—
．．．．．．．．．．．．．．．．．reprise in her head
her reply an hour ago to the man
who wanted to buy her house,
who said, *It must've been a dream home
when you built it*, that yes, she'd always said
her husband would have to bury her
in the backyard because she'd never leave.

Deeper still, the memory of that June afternoon
rises up like her husband's chest, pushing
through doors, plowing into her, his hands
threshing the phone
．．．．．．．．．．．．．．．．．．from her fingers
trying to dial 9-1-1. Her eventual escape,
locking herself in her bathroom, calling
for help. His text later on, oblivious
to apology, saying he'd come back
to mow the lawn. The restraining order.

Then: her packing his things, pulling
sweaters from their year-long cocoons,
shoes from their sockets, wondering
if her tears would dry, once & for all,
like a creek accepting its fate
after rain's desertion.
All she knows is
      the sudden jerk
& her grasp on the leash. She hangs on
beneath the barley moon.

PTSD

The counselor tells the wife to write through fear,
mine her journal's thirty-thousand words
for the hardest rocks to remove, embedded
so deep in trauma's obsidian-black cave,
no sensible chisel can cut them free,
the husband's endless indictments convincing her
she must be *ridiculous*, her every need *absurd*.

The therapist also says to revise
the script of her recurring nightmare,
take the six-foot figure of her husband
barreling into her as she tries to hold
every door, laughing at her when she says,
You are scaring me (the predictable sequence
inspired by her marriage's last day),

& turn it into a kitten,
reduce his ridicule to one meager
meow. Once the wife gets going,
she goes even further, withdrawing
its claws, extracting its twenty-six teeth,
feeding its feeble form nothing
but the cream it craves.

Once,

after her husband soaked begonias
    in their early autumn beds

& drenched ferns suspended
    high above the porch, misting,

as he went, white balustrade,
    rocking chairs, & her;

after he doused pink impatiens by the door
    & puddles formed & one narrow

tributary streamed
    toward the stoop, trickled

over; after he stowed away the hose
    & sparrows filled the still-

green pear tree, their noise
    a veritable storm of story;

then
    evening's blue deluge

deepened, hushing the birds,
    & all was resonance:

water's sweet chemistry
    rustling leaves & petals,

earth's soft swallows.
    Soft, the earth swallows

leaves & petals, sweet
    chemistry rustling

with water, resonating
    through birds, deepening

in evening's blue deluge,
    this veritable storm of story

unlike a green pear tree,
    sparrow-filled.

Long ago, the noise stilled
    after he stowed away the hose.

What trickles over the stoop now,
    what streams in the tributary

from a puddle by the door,
    from pink impatiens, doused?

Rocking chairs, white balustrade,
    her,

all beneath mist high above the porch,
    where ferns suspend

their thirst for summer,
    for that husband

soaking begonias in their bed, once.

In a parallel universe,

which some physicists say may exist,
perhaps the husband actually asks

for forgiveness, head bowed,
confessing his offenses,

giving them their proper names—
this being one alternative

on a quantum scale that doesn't mean
how it sounds—not epic, but *small*.

Then again, when she stares at memory's
polychromatic walls, she thinks of Pollock's

full-bodied swirls, how they imitate
the same geometry of galaxies,

& wonders whether her existence
preceded its essence, or the other way around,

while she walks along the floors of her future,
the night sky, her roof,

Earth's lone moon, her window,
God's good stars, particles

of light in the only life she knows.

Full Long Nights Moon

Sitting on his bench, the judge splits
the union on December's hard grounds,
frozen deep as the circles under her ex-
husband's eyes,
                eyes she can no longer meet
as she bows her head & the frigid hand
of heartbreak grips her
again—
        O, this is the vows' un-
doing, as if the wedding song
were rewinding, revealing the back-
masking of promises, their code no longer
hidden, as it was twenty-seven years ago now,

when she thought their love
could cast out fear,
when the high June sun
was the only thing
that made them sweat.
                They're left
with the full long nights moon
whose voice will hover
above the horizon tonight,
moaning in the wind,
its bleak, blue breath
substantial as stone.

Aftershock

Full Worm Moon

Sap Moon, Crust Moon, Crow Moon—
by any of its names, this moon
announces, in all its fullness, worms
stirring in earth's softening center;
sap thawing in maples;
snow dissolving by day, crisping by night;
& crow calls converting from haunting ballads
to heralding hymns. A robin reappears,
throwing off the pine cloak it hid behind
all winter like a god hard to find, hard to hear,
maybe hard of hearing in the ruckus
wind made as it bayed across plains
& yowled down valleys, hard to see in ice
suffocating once-tasseled fields, pinecone & bayberry,
numbing perhaps even wings,
rendering the soft touch this moon offers
almost senseless.   Welcome, worms,
twisting & teeming with prophecy;
welcome, crows & robins, plucking
them from grass now breathing green;
welcome, syrup, born again, pushing through the spout;
welcome, waxing light & waning dark;
welcome one, welcome all, no matter your longing
for answered prayer, come, sun yourself
beneath the low Lenten Moon.

Mailbox

Rivers of Ohio rain cascaded
    into March, flooding streams & roads,
        then turned, one evening,

into snow, despite the 36 degrees
    & the way the groundhog,
        one month before, had missed his shadow.

So bending by the road,
    I picked up my mailbox
        knocked down once again

by snow swept into it, the plow's force
    strong enough to push
        a person over, but not really

massive, the favorite word
    that morning as the media described
        the 9.0 quake in Japan, the ensuing

tsunami. The axis of the whole world
    shifted several inches, they told us,
        shortening the day by 1.8 microseconds,

unlike Joshua's lingering sun.
    No horns signaled heroic victory.
        No moon refused to rise.

The dark storm of radiation
    loomed above like a god gone awry,
        while some kneeled in water, or snow,

begging for a word of explanation.

Palm Sunday

As rain pounds the pavement,
my father, mother, & I sip our soup
at Tim Horton's after church
where their choir sang of triumphal

entry, death, & resurrection.
Somehow, our conversation turns
to my grandfather, a gambling man,
a carpenter who lost half his thumb

to a saw but shuffled cards like a pro,
riffling them so they'd intertwine,
smoothly, like the fingers of a supplicant,
then building a bridge where cards

fell on their faces into one neat deck.
My dad remembers nights
my grandmother sent my uncle
to find his father, ensnared

in another game—the poker
he'd picked up while playing
hockey for the Toronto St. Pats,
always trying to relive the year

he won it all, a defenseman
who collected the Stanley Cup.
I visualize his picture hanging
in the Halifax Hockey Hall of Fame:

Tall in uniform, steady
on his skates. How did he fall,
become the man who threw
grocery money into the pot?

How did he conjure the nerve
to call my father after he was married
with three kids of his own, desperation
straining through the receiver,

to beg for a loan? Did my grandfather
wince when my dad said, *No,
I know you'll lose it all*?
What does that do to a man

like my dad who worked two jobs,
logging 60-hour weeks,
so we could live in Moorestown
where the schools were good?

What does it do to a man to tell his father *No*?
Does the son carry the word's wound
all his life, feel it even now, thirty years
after his father's death, as his broth grows cold?

Aftershock

People may be able to go much longer without a pulse than the 20 minutes previously believed. The capnograph, which measures carbon dioxide being expelled from the mouth of the patient, can tell rescuers when further efforts at cardiopulmonary resuscitation . . . should be continued.
–Wall Street Journal, May 17, 2011

*I'm a regular guy. I happened to die
at the right place at the right time,*
said Howard Snitzer after he was revived.

Ninety-six minutes he spent without a pulse
lying in front of a grocery store while Mayo medics
worked on him, using a capnograph

to gauge how his lungs clung to longer life.

In that hour & a half, did his soul wander
down to the banks of the Acheron River,
chat with Charon, who refused to ferry him

to the other side, immediately knowing, as he did,
that Howard was neither dead man
nor tragic hero, no Aeneas, for example, bearing

golden branch & the burden of a nation's destiny?

When asked what he was doing there,
did Howard shrug his shoulders
& shove his hands into his disembodied

pockets, then jangle those immaterial
coins the cashier gave him
after purchasing milk, bread, & eggs?

How impatient did Charon grow

as he counted like strikes of a clock the echoes
of defibrillator shocks—twelve in all—
rocking his usually steady boat?

Is this the story Charon now tells every spirit
he takes for a ride—how the water
throbbed beneath his feet, how in the end,

he rubbed his eyes in disbelief?

Comet

What on Earth were you thinking?
    my mother yelled as she grabbed the ipecac syrup,
        served me a spoonful, & yanked
my wrist, dragging me to the bathroom.

What indeed. Swirl of green in a Dixie cup.
    Froth like I'd seen on moon-
        induced waves licking
the Jersey shore. Stirring

with a spoon, I'd concocted
    my courage over the laundry sink
        while my sister & brother watched,
saying, *Betcha can't do it.*

I sipped, sampling bile & sand,
    the solution's caustic point,
        which usually proved its power
in my mother's hands, scouring

black rings around tubs,
    mildew from tile.
        Rufus, our first dog,
lying on the linoleum,

Shepherd lungs still filling with air,
    witnessed the whole thing.
        What did the animal
of my girl-body know then?

Even my blood hadn't yet issued
    forth, pulsing, as it was,
        in its elliptical orbit, blue cells
streaking in their dark & unseen sphere.

I was led to believe

you could swallow your tongue
one day waiting for a matinee
with my father, sister, & brother—

the line long, stretching out the door—
as we anticipated the lasers & space ships
we'd heard about in *Star Wars*—

when another fan ahead of us,
on the other side of the room,
near the heavy, red drapes,

collapsed.
         My dad, a pharmacist,
asked everyone in earnest

for a pencil or popsicle stick,
then incarnated the myth,
sliding wood between the woman's teeth.

I'd already learned by then
how to fool my family,
finding coins I'd stolen in places

where I myself had hid them,
knew, too, how a President's pretense
could turn a nation's mouth sour.

But I didn't yet know you could instill
a lie, believing it sincerely to be true.
It'd be years before I'd learn

how the tongue of Cicero, cooling
after decapitation, suffered the insult
of a hair pin—Fulvia's persistent stabs.

How later, the Romans,
when they entered the Forum
then saw his head & hands,

red & heavy,
                      nailed to the Rostra,
perceived, as Plutarch tells,

the likeness of Antony's very soul.
How they shuttered their ears,
swallowed their republican tongues.

Where were you when you realized

your mother would one day die?
I was in my living room reading about Stephen Dedalus
as Baby Tuckoo, unable to remember if I ever wet my bed,
though I could recall, long ago, posting my little sister at the edge
of the boxwood hedge to spy anyone approaching
before I peed in my neighbor's bushes on Church Street,
using an oak leaf for the wiping.

My mother was busy making dinner,
maybe noodles boiling in a pot,
sauce simmering, ground beef sizzling—
all for Hungarian goulash,
a dish I hated, the too-many, too-mushy tomatoes
mingling with the meat, triggering nausea
like a finger inching toward the back of my throat—

when I walked into the kitchen to ask her,
with all the transparency a teen dare muster,
Will you die? One day. Will you?
She, wondering what in the world
the school was doing to me that week,
shrugged off my question as she picked up
the paprika, flavored what she could.

Strawberry Moon

In memoriam, Michele Patterson, 1964-2014

The moon is not, as Donovan once sang,
a typical lady, certainly not that year's full
June moon, Celtic Moon of Horses,
Choctaw Windy Moon,

Friday-the-13th moon carrying
usual promise of green corn & red berries
with unusual anniversary—
my twenty-seventh year of marriage

marked by terminal separation.
That same night my friend
wrote me about her diagnosis,
tentacles of glioblastoma winding

through her brain cells—
her toppling over in her closet
& right leg solo-marching at work
just the beginning

of the end I would sense
five months later, in early November,
when I sat in her family room,
her Christmas tree festooned with lights,

which she admired from her wheelchair.
We wondered how our lives
had turned so suddenly
sour, how long ago, our milk

spilled from our strawberry nipples,
satisfying our children, born
within months of each other,
who became best friends,

how grief now invaded
like vines, twisting in our throats,
as she told me she'd almost lost
hope, those last words

I ever heard her speak
echoing in the chambers
of my heart, in each stage of the final
good-byes we had to brave.

No Heaven

Come, all you who are thirsty, come to the waters; and you who have no money, come, buy and eat! Come, buy wine and milk without money and without cost. Why spend money on what is not bread, and your labor on what does not satisfy? Listen, listen to me, and eat what is good, and your soul will delight in the richest of fare.
—Isaiah 55: 1-3

Let us pause in life's pleasures & count its many tears,

Hard rain, flash floods,
green sky, ball-sized hail,
earthquake, tsunami,
bodies, bodies—

While we all sup sorrow with the poor;

capitalism, Marxism—
does it really matter which
to the mom who gives up her baby
to adoption, or abortion,

There's a song that will linger forever in our ears;

because she can't afford
a cup of milk, or any good book,
& can't wait any longer for Isaiah's
invitation to arrive?

Oh hard times, come again no more.

She figures it got lost in the mail,
or was never meant for her anyway.

    There's a pale drooping maiden who toils her life away,

The woman wrapped
in her pimp's unending
covenant, one she didn't ask for
when snatched, years ago,

    With a worn heart whose better days are o'er.

from her Haitian village
amid her daily chore,
pail filled with water,
left behind, spilling out.

    Though her voice would be merry, 'tis sighing all the day,

Displayed beneath Amsterdam's red lights,
in a shop window,
she stands with other women plucked
from poverty's tangled vines.

    Oh, hard times, come again no more.

Or the man, memory of his priest's private
part impeding his reach for the bread of life,

    While we seek mirth & beauty & music light & gay,

boy within searching,
always, for salvation.
Another boy, this one
hammering the quarry in India,

There are frail forms fainting at the door;

feeling as if the rocks were embedded
in his back, his arms & legs electric
with agony, his labor never satisfying
his owner, his father, himself.

Though their voices are silent, their pleading looks will say

O, the kidnapped girls in Nigeria—
if we can't hear them dropping
to the ground, one by one,
like pines in a Maine forest,

Oh, hard times, come again no more.

does that mean they no longer exist,
or their fate is not tragic or true?

'Tis the song, the sigh of the weary,

Can you hear ethnic cleansing's anthem groaning?
If we scrub people from the Earth like mildew,
do the promises disappear, too?
What deliverance for the Sudanese?

Hard Times, hard times, come again no more.

Is there no heaven for them?
No heaven for we who devour
our processed cheese, our genetically
modified organisms, our empty, homegrown

Many days you have lingered around my cabin door;

headlines, distracting ourselves to the point
of everyone's death?
Tell me, Isaiah, tell me now,
how do any of us eat what is good,

    Oh, hard times, come again no more.

what will last? Teach us how to hear God
over all the noise—the chisel, the sword,

    'Tis a sigh that is wafted across the troubled wave,

even the tornado's plow
in small Cedarville, Ohio
through the century-old farmhouse,
the barns, the silos.

    'Tis a wail that is heard upon the shore

Show us how the cries of the farmer
& his family, rising
with their roof as their once-
dependable walls fall,

    'Tis a dirge that is murmured around the lowly grave

trapping them in the basement,
beneath the rubble of several generations,
are heard as firefighters free them,
& volunteers then work the fields

    Oh, hard times come again no more.

to salvage what they can—
hearing aids, wedding band, Bible.

Barn Burning

My neighbor tends the circle of fire
on the floor where the stables once stood.

Planks were loose & warped, paint
splintered, faded like a memory,
tin roof sunken,

threatening, always, to come down.

Every time the wind would whirl,
the whole thing rattled,

so she'd say to me, like a mother
whisking away a disruptive child,
I'm so sorry about that.

This summer, she summonsed a bulldozer

to tear half of it down in a single day.
She stands in its place now,

igniting wood that once housed her father's
hay & cows, their former way of life
flickering, spectral,

rising with the smoke.

Reflex

I have a dangerous habit. Whenever a stone or bird smacks my windshield, I blink. I close my eyes on impact. I do not choose this. I should be vision-rich when it happens. Aware. Steady. Ready to respond. Instead, I'm in the dark. Unable to recognize if I'm heading off the road or crossing lanes. Stunned. Like when someone says something outrageous. A lie, for instance. I sit there. Like I've been slapped in the face & must smooth the swift hand's burn. I can't conjure a word, not a single letter appears before me. Blind but not blind. Impaired. As the debris of deception falls everywhere around me.

Orb Weaver

So much depends on the fine line it spins,
how its very life hangs
in the balance between calm & wind,
between distance from the porch floor

& proximity to my door,
between the patience it exhibits in its still legs
as it waits all day to snare a moth
& the way it works up its spider-sweat

as it wraps its silk rope around the wings, lets
its venom go. Later, when the moment's heat
has past, it enjoys its meal, a hexagon then
heavy with triumph, suspended

there in the entry where I stand,
my broom in my hand.

Cooper's Hawks

Santa Fe National Forest

Where Atalaya Trail meets tiny tributaries
formed by El Niño's leaky faucets,

two black pines rise, stirring
with Cooper's Hawks, one in each tree,

their barrel-breasts heaving
as they fan their blue-gray wings

& shake their black-banded tail feathers,
acting like self-important sentinels on a break

jabbering about the chance of rain
or the next meal they aim to hunt, soaring

above the sagebrush as they do,
searching for birds to snatch & squeeze to death.

They seem to think God put them here,
long ago, after mountain & desert,

before man & woman, while ants populated
their intricate colonies, a wonder

these birds have never noticed,
sky swimmers & leaf loungers that they are,

the soil to them a mystery
as deep as a moonless night,

the very thing they never mention.

Coming Close

Mule deer gather
in the Strawberry Valley,
feeding as the moon
in its white robe
nudges the sun, drowsing
along the horizon, to bed.

The animals allow
my daughter & me
to come close,
one snorting, yes,
but the other five
looking up, nerves mute,

sounding no senseless
alarm, then lowering
their mouths to the meadow,
the grass's old familiar tune
fading in, humming
on all our tongues.

Following the Light

On Grand River, by Frank Weston Benson, c. 1920

High noon, the water bright as the idea
the man had thirty minutes ago
when he launched his canoe,
alone, long wooden pole in hand,
flinging his life vest onto the seat,
seeking nothing but a certain slant
of light, not even a single fish,
in the middle of summer in 1920
& the Grand River:

Behind him is another life,
maybe a wife, maybe children,
wondering where he's off to now,
prone to wander as he often is,
not far from home, never
in an untrue manner,
but still, disappearing on days like this
once the urgent work is finished,
glint in his eye giving him away

to the old dog, the only one
who catches him as he
grabs his hat & heads out back.
The hound knows this is no hunting trip
into the woods, no trek up the mountainside,
knows to stay put & return to his dreams
of raccoon chases & bones buried
within reach. What the man does
in the canoe is a balancing act:

As the blue-tailed damselflies flit & flash,
he hunches, slides the pole to the mud below
then pushes down, pushes forward,
pursuing Monet's palette
of yellow, green, orange, purple—
and blue in every hue—
all rippling in the pines on the shoreline
& farther still, in the current yet to come,
something swift, something slow.

Walking on the Roof

St. Meinrad Archabbey

My son & I walk on the roof of the library
on a pebble path along the perimeter,

the way so narrow, we have to go in single file,
straight ahead, then right, then right again.

Grass & weeds grow wildly within,
wet from the recent rain that rinsed away

this July day's horizontal heat.
Like a labyrinth, the trail insists

on being followed, though we expect
no great reward or revelation,

though we know nothing will greet us
at the end except some sense of completion,

or solace, if we're lucky.
As we go along, the words of a monk,

whom I passed by at last night's
wine & cheese reception,

rise up to meet me,
posing once again his question:

*If you dive into a pool with no water, you just turn
around & walk back onto the board, right?*

I consider the many books below, how many letters
of saints or words of poetry

by Virgil or Dante or Milton may reverberate
between the walls & emerge like worms

through the soil somehow fertile & contained.
Here, it's not possible to change

direction without breaking stride,
without breaking a sort of vow

to finish what we started.

Milton

–for Peggy Wilfong

Truth is strong.... She needs no policies, nor stratagems, nor licensings to make her victorious; those are the shifts and the defences that error uses against her power. Give her but room, and do not bind her when she sleeps...
                              –Areopagitica

Every morning, long before sunrise,
a single bird blows its tiny whistle—

not sparrow or dove or chickadee,
a bird I cannot name scientifically—

its praise a will-o'-the-wisp might sing,
if it ever got its wish—

challenging darkness to a duel
for striking other voices down,

a signature tune insisting meekly,
Give me room and do not bind me while I sleep.

I lie in bed, listening to this native tongue
(its will no act of God can bend

or school of night erase),
gathering notes of gold in this unlikely place.

Morning Prayer

God bless the cow in the field that sneezes.
    God bless the dog who hears the sneeze,

then lunges, at play, toward the fence.
    God bless the gold finch landing on that fence,

perching between barbs on the wire.
    God bless the farmer who works the wire,

who woke early to heave wet soil from the place
    it slid to overnight. God bless this place

as I wander through, cattails gleaming in first light,
    frogs humming their last song of moonlight.

God bless the song, welcome as grain
    in the old trough, while yesterday's rain

swells in the brook, an old hymn hallowing the break
    of day, finch now flitting over the cattle, breaking away.

Blackberry Seeds

I didn't cry when my great grandfather died twenty years ago.
That suddenly comes to mind when I clear the haze
of slumber from my head, sipping coffee,
gazing at the fog, thick as snow, & the sheep

meandering through it like they, too, just emerged
from sleep. When I see the spider webs on my deck
shrouded in frost, stiff in the breeze,
my tears blossom like memory.

How clearly the Poconos,
once home to my great grandfather,

reappeared. I inhaled that air again,
clean as white lilies, crisp as mint.
We sat on the back porch,
my sister, brother, & I, playing monopoly,

chewing on caramels, listening to the low tones
of Johnny Cash. Uncle Herb was there, too,
tending to his trains from his wheel chair,
clacking his loose dentures, his jaw moving like a nutcracker's.

The mountains leaned toward the windows,
whispering words I couldn't discern.

Grandfather Harris, with his plaid flannel shirt
tucked into his trousers, hair white as cotton,
nose red yes, as a cherry, spoke something about deer—
how they would gather in the long grass

down the hill—their breath steaming from their nostrils—
then dash—their tails like white blips bounding
across the green radar screen of his land.
Oh, how he loved to show us their black turds in the woods,

wild blackberries along the logging road, & black bear
when it rambled through! How he wanted us to marvel.

This explained our bouncy rides on his Farmall tractor, the long stems
flashing fuchsia in his rhubarb patch, & the way he'd offer
apples like blessings from his McIntosh tree. Why the water
pumped by his hand tasted like awe, like it had just sprung

from rock. Why no matter what thicket we wandered into,
what weeds grasped our ankles, or what howls we heard at dusk,
he knew we were never lost. Why we popped those berries
into our mouths, swallowed the seeds.

Why we believed, like my dad often teased,
something would sprout within us.

There Is No Violence Here

What do birches teach us,
their yellow leaves long ago
having tumbled to the ground,
exposing limbs to whatever raw
& consequential wind
may come? Trunks stippled
with dark eyes. Branches now
boasting only the robust breasts
of crows. I will not mention roots.
This is not about them,
those long siphons stretching
toward water's deep horizon.
Look closer. See the lenticels
scattered across the white bark.
They look like scars, as if a cold
blade striated the surface. But no,
they are not slits in the trees' bloodless
throats. (There is no violence here.)
They are pores oxygen slides through
as simply & surely as sunlight
slips through a spider's silk net.
Lean in. Listen to the soft
cellular breath tell you what it can.

Moon When Horns Are Broken Off

Clouds rush in at dusk, rolling
                        the moon sideways,
      a sight as dizzying as lightning
    reeling in this November sky,
            disembodied as thunder on the ground,
that terra firma where the hunter
                readies for the weeks close at hand,
        tightening his bow, oiling his rifle
     for the time when the buck
                  will stand in the hollow
just before dawn,
     silent & unseeing,
         its breath an ethereal veil
                one well-placed shot
will tear asunder.
        When its seeds spill forth,
    red & terrible, birthing a pool
slick with whatever the man wants to call it—
                chicanery? precision? pure luck?—
its antlers
       will not lie in the woods
               for mice to gnaw
                      all winter long,
    but will hang
  still attached atop their head
    on a wooden wall,
          bloodless bones
                 bound to outlast
                          the man below.

Easy Prey

I am eating stroganoff
    made with seasoned meat
        from a bison my friend has slaughtered,

not in some Wyoming outpost
    but here in southwest Ohio
        just minutes from my home.

A farmer there keeps a herd,
    allows a few hunters each November
        to enter the field, cull the population.

You see, the bull is polygamous,
    the females, a harem,
        their steady stream

of calves a clear threat
    to the grasses they graze.
        So the arrow slung

pierces more than just a tender
    lung, steals more
        than one beast's breath.

Before the cow
    drops to her knees,
        her blood drains

onto the stubs of corn stalks,
    drawing the animals around her.
        When her legs finally

give way, into a bull's eye
    of bodies they crowd,
        bowing before her,

their horns prying her head
    from the ground,
        trying to coax her

to her feet. In the wilderness,
    long ago, when they gathered
        around such loss,

they were always easy
    prey, their instincts
        leading them astray.

Close Range

In memoriam, Elizabeth Carter, 1965-2012

A sopping day in December, & warm as May,
    spawned a thousand millipedes on my porch,

each one crawling like a small wave, so as a whole,
    the cement seemed to ripple.

This was the day, two miles away, in your home,
    your husband fired first at you, then at his own

mad head. That night, the millipedes swarmed.
    As I crossed the concrete to plug in our lights,

there was nowhere to step that was free
    from their figures, vulnerable beneath my feet.

I wondered if you curled the length
    of your body in defense, hoping the aim's close

range wouldn't matter & the shot would miss,
    so your sons would never witness this leaden hour,

would hug instead, in their usual way,
    your slender shoulders as they'd walk out the door

into the rain—car keys in hand, coats unzipped,
    no silhouettes in their path.

Present

Fog obscures December sun,
diffusing light all day long,
so evening's now a haze
for this year's Little Town of Lights.
Luminaries line the sidewalks
as villagers saunter from shop
to shop, clutching cookies and hot drinks.
The local café sells roasted beans
for $9 a package, the church distributes
small, wooden crèches in Ziploc bags,
and the senior center boasts
homemade crafts and Santa's fat lap.
Unaccompanied by child or spouse,
I walk toward the open house
that brings me out.
It's not loneliness I feel
as I buy coffee and greet the woman
I've known for years. Not sadness
as families pass, toddlers in tow
with candy canes sticking to their fingers.
What I sense is my singularity
dimming my vision,
subtle as a strand of hair
and its nearly imperceptible brush
with skin, not painful
but present all the same,
and slightly out of place.

The Road My Daughter Drives On

It's too easy to say life is like a flake
    of snow, fragile, susceptible

to the elements—
    heat, for instance, when molecules

dissolve like sugar on a tongue
    & thaw on asphalt hoarding

the fervor of yesterday's sun.
    Or arctic air, perhaps,

which particles ride like resentment
    while they build whole shorelines of ice.

But that is what I think as I watch
    white & weightless crystals,

horizontal in the wind,
    accumulate on the ground

& melt on the road my daughter drives on,
    my son her passenger,

as they head home,
    depending on the boundaries

blurred between earth's warm
    reception & cold clarity,

exposed, as we all are, to separation's
    fluctuating degrees.

Nest in a Winter Tree

Wing 5, Colorado Yule Marble, by Elizabeth Turk, 1998

Near the winter solstice, amid a maple's taciturn timber
    here on my snow-marbled lawn,

sits a nest, like a sparrow once did.
    How could Plato believe

we'd fallen from once-heavenly flights,
    unglued, as we'd supposedly become, from our glory?

This persevering nest seems to thrum
    upon the stripped bones of solitude.

A moon-silver feather, like a bow,
    could play the air's tender strings,

sliding, side to side,
    as it reaches for land.

So tell me: What body,
    whole or broken,

doesn't have the soul of that song
    swelling in its breast?

Molasses

After twisting open the lid on the jar of molasses,
I raise the glass, inhale the earthy aroma,
part bark, part root of everyone
who gave me breath.
                        Comes my great grandmother Elsie,
her round body & gray hair pinned neatly in place,
her red gingham dress & rhubarb pies,
her Lebkuchen cookies. Her heart
the only day it failed, hours before my parents
caught us jumping on our beds & sat us down.
The first darkness of my childhood
pouring thickly over me.
                        Comes my grandmother Irma,
her dyed-blond hair & lanky frame,
her lemon meringue pies,
job at Motown Records in Jersey,
slipping vinyl discs into sleeves.
Her back broken from osteoporosis,
her lungs smothered
in the black gum of night.
                        Comes my mother Doris,
the brunette curls, hazel eyes, & wide hips
she gave me, her left-handed pitcher's arm,
loud laughter, banana bread, & yes, those Christmas
cookies. The high blood pressure she fears
will, in some future year,
cast a long viscous shadow
over her words, still her limbs.

                        They are all here
as I mix the syrup with flour & sugar,
nutmeg & cloves, as I roll, cut, & bake
the deep brown dough.
Dusted white by day's end,
I seem to walk with them
through rooms imbued
with the heart's heady scent.

In Which the Magpie Resurrects the Voice of Henry David Thoreau

The Magpie, by Claude Monet, 1868-69

I am the magpie, sitting atop the wattle fence.
I embody the snow that fell overnight
& blue shadows cast by morning sun—
the fence's & the great trees' & yes, mine
all resting there on Normandy's ground.
I know the woman you can't see in the butter-colored house
who boils carrots & parsnips over the fire
& the invisible man who plows the field beyond me
in the spring. I stretch forth my black breast,
impressed that I can perch here,
or fly, depending on my need.
Once, a long time ago, I sailed through
a rainbow, & its light tinged my wings green,
so all summer long, I sang of solitude.
Still, loss sometimes weighs upon my shoulders
(though I have no quarrel with God),
as when a brother dies & I gather with others
to walk around the body & wail.
Those essentials I encounter often,
like now, for instance, as the violet mist
dissipates, I spy another man close by,
the one with a brush in his hand.
I imagine he will practice on his pale canvas
anything but resignation.

This Is the Landscape Left

Objects in Mirror Are Closer Than They Appear

Unlike the cardinal
at my car's side mirror
this past summer,
who found there
dark eyes & red, menacing feathers,
provoking it (so certain of its instincts)
to beak & claw the glass,
this harvest moon
doesn't seem deceived.
It has the gift of distance.
It gazes into my neighbor's pond,
gleaming like one enamored
with her own reflection,
its alabaster surface so close
I want to lower my hand
into the black water & swirl
the image till it loses all sense
of proportion, so when I leave,
light will drip from my fingertips.

Ode to a Pumpkin Patch Discovered By a Trail

Rocky Fork State Park, Hillsboro, Ohio

      O, burnished gourds formed, illusion-like,
   from flowers fluted & bright as Sun Ray Lilies,
     you who emerge small as fists, green as an Irish meadow,
who don't need much forethought or tending

      to spring up or wax moon-like,
   moon-lit in the square acre you claimed
     with your forlorn seeds that survived
last year's flesh, rotten as it became

      till it melted into dew, you seem to want
   for nothing, to spread your vines
     like spiders stretch their silk,
invisibly—as if from nowhere it arrives

      & only becomes known when chanced upon
   in an unweeded garden. Your oblong orbs,
     your world of worlds spinning
your cells on your axis, your pulp

      plump with promise to the teeth
   that bit into you & left their marks,
     something wild that toted or rolled
one of you from your patch,

      leaving you there on the trail,
  as though you were too tough, too early
     to satisfy any purpose but prestidigitation,
appearing from the wave of some enchanted hand.

Hope

It's the Iris bulbs my mother excavates
when her house sells in early December,
salvaging the purple & yellow flags
she wants to see waving
on my lawn come June.

It's every uneven form,
rough & robust & ugly
as any root you can name—
rutabaga, radish, turnip, or beet—
ready to ripen in a pot of stew.

It's each small space I hollow,
swinging wide warm-autumn weeds,
lowering life like a pail
where it stays till it feels
the tug, then rises.

Science Lesson

The door didn't glow gold last night when you un-
    locked it, when you pushed it out of the way
        & the long blue hallway stretched
            before you. The hallway wasn't blue either.

That cantaloupe you plucked
    from the chandelier & sliced into wedges
        wasn't orange, or pink,
            but pale as your spoon.

You were dreaming.
    Science says those acrobats
        of the rainbow can't swing
            on your retina when your lids fall

into the net of sleep.
    For veiled in white (so the lesson goes),
        the promise of every hue is wed like hope
            to the sun's every glimmer. They cross

the threshold together.
    One can't go without the other
        into the tar-dark room of slumber.
            There, deep below the land

of light, the colors in the spectrum
    stay silent as silver, invisible as glass.
        So that purple house you entered,
            those chartreuse curtains on the windows,

    those tiles kaleidoscopic on the kitchen floor—
        they were just blips in your brain waves.
            The logic seems tight as a knot,
                secure as a system of knowledge.

Still, what dreams
    do come, what clever eye
        the mind opens, following
            every electric ray.

The Philosopher & the Poet Talk on the Last Warm Day in Fall

—for Steve Broidy

My neighbor scrapes old paint
from the fence around his pasture,
an annual chore he attends to,
for he knows the white he applies
preserves each board.
                      I think of his recent essay,
peeling back the layers, as he said,
of online education, revealing a barren base
devoid of the body's subtle
gestures—
           how a screen cannot replicate
confusion written on a brow,
engagement flashing in the eyes,
or a hand touching a shoulder.
How a cursor cannot translate
the voice's inflections, nuanced
as the nod of his head, greeting me,
while he lays
           down his tool to rub my dog's ears,
while he motions toward the remaining wood,
tells how he'll finish the job before winter.

The Problem with School

My son's friend likes Shakespeare
but hates school. Emmett's a rough neck,
a red neck, a trampoline-jumping,
video-game-thumping player.
He's read *Hamlet* & *Macbeth*.
Thinks they're cool. But damnèd
Ds adorn his report card
like spells on the breath of witches
or stubborn spots on a lady's hands.
So when their teacher assigns a paper
to discuss a book
the students have never read,
Emmett picks *Hamlet*.
But you already read that,
my son with his ethics in tow
& confident 4.0 says.
I know, Emmett says, his brilliant
method burning through the mask
of his matter-of-fact madness.
She'd never believe it.

Piano Lesson

There's no room, no space to rent in this town,
Bono croons, as I wait in my car
for my son, who's finishing his piano lesson

inside his teacher's house. The time slips
past nine, & the moon, hidden
behind winter clouds, holds back its light.

I'm worn thin as long-worked linen
under the hand of another dean
who's unaware of the sublime,

who doesn't celebrate the faculty
of two minds, side by side, discovering
transcendence in an ancient verse.

Through the window,
through its sheer drapes,
I see my son, his back swaying,

his fingers ascending
& descending the keyboard,
concerto no doubt resounding

with the same brave spirit he summons
at home. I love this town,
but I'm tired of negotiating boundaries

for beauty, of being an annoying
voice among the professions, crying,
like Rilke, *You must change your life.*

What if the beautiful day is over?
I wonder as my son now ends his piece,
gathers together his music sheets,

& heads toward the door.
What if all that remains is the measure
of loss, the last chord struck

amid the surrounding silence?

Lament

—Lamentations 3:28-29

Someone strikes a minor chord
on the piano in your head
when you see red on the snow
where it doesn't belong—
                              this is no holly berry
or Cardinal feather, no,
this is your beloved Lab,
thirteen years into her life,
squatting, bleeding *from a vessel
split open, perhaps by a walnut swallowed
in haste,* the vet will say later, *or a tumor
beginning its hemorrhage.*

Here, now, you bend low and hold her,
the chord now a prayer,
then a memory of the birthday
when your children and husband
gave you Maggie,
                    a million songs ago,
a million walks and wishes past,
back when he loved you, when he swore

to God he would *have and hold*,
before your once-safe life, like your womb,
transformed
               into wound—
that morning you woke
to find it festering,
and you sat alone in silence,
waiting, with something like dust
thickening in your mouth.

Certainty

It's the one thing you're sure doesn't exist. Everyone agrees. Mostly. Its absence like a kid disappearing from class, the one who used to sit beside you till she walked her dog one night & vanished. Of course you know she's missing. You feel her not-being-there like you sense a ghost. No. Not a ghost. Something intangible but real as a thorn. The thing you can touch but don't want to when you think about it. The thing you can taste. Metal. Salt. Dirt. Not ice cream or chocolate. Maybe something substantive, though, something complex, like rutabaga or parsnip. Something at the root of things. It scares you a little that sometimes, you find the loss a little comforting. (It was someone else's pretty sister.) You can still go to college. Get married. Get a job. Pay taxes like everyone. Your death is a long way off. You're banking on it. This is the hope you sleep with. Slipped under your pillow like a tooth. When oak branches don't scrape against the window. When shadows don't dance on the ceiling. When darkness is a friend you're positive won't stab you in the back.

Cryoseism

Frost quakes, rare phenomena that simulate earthquakes, rattled hundreds of residents Thursday in Darke and Miami counties in Ohio and Randolph County in Indiana, emergency management officials said.

 —*Dayton Daily News*, February 11, 2011

No, they do not simulate earthquakes at all,
not the kind that rocked Japan to its core,
split wide the ocean floor & shot, fast
as a jet, its deep waters to the closest
& farthest shores, drowning mothers & fathers,
children, cousins, & friends. Noisy yes,
the explosions rose from beneath the layers
of ice & snow, as liquid seeped below,
then froze, expanded, stressing rocks
till something had to pop. Sure, residents
were scared. But not to death.
Just one moment of fright,
harmless as a horror movie, Godzilla
unreal, even melodramatic, his long tail
swinging into buildings, his roar
reminiscent of a good hard laugh.
So what if some siding wriggled
loose or a shingle fell from the roof,
if some man ran buck naked out his front
door to see what the hell had shaken his house?
He returned to his tub, warmed himself
in the shower, & when he finished,
he did what all of us want to do,
turned that water off.

What If Feels Like,

reads the chart the weatherman
shows on Fox45 News at 10,
unaware of the typo as he tells

how arctic gusts, howling-
hoarse here in Ohio tonight,
feel on our skin. I think

yes, this is what *if* feels like,
not *if* I had a million dollars
or *if* I could do anything I wanted,

but that icier state of the subjunctive mood:

If I were you, I wouldn't do that fill-
in-the-blank behavior, *say*, work
that thankless job or marry that loser

or raise that existential question.
No, definitely don't ask, the wind-
chilled whisper warns. Keep your mouth

closed, so you can stay where you are,
settling like snow, only believing
in what you can measure.

The Conversation of Wood

Across the street, the barn,
half-razed & hanging tough
since last summer,
has come undone.

The tin roof, despite its protests,
finally surrendered.
Wrenched free while hinges
hollered, the door now

lies upon the lawn.
Beams & joists bowed
to long-winded pressure
while rain's cruel voice

injected itself, time & again,
into the conversation of wood
once engineered with civility.
This is how it rots:

A few suspicions sour
the tongues in their grooves
& breed. Then: the rafters
no longer seem righteous.

Blood Moon

Beneath this April's full moon,
an inch of snow fell, eclipsing

daffodils & tulips, their budding
genius. Cherry blossoms wear

white gowns now, shivering
as they somehow—is it possible?—

become more beautiful, as if the cold's shock
rocks their simple, pink world,

spurring metamorphosis beyond
the binaries of winter-spring,

bleakness-promise, cocoon-
wing. They move into a third space

hospitable for another life
more rare, more raw.

This is the landscape left

Night Forest, 18" x 24," mixed media on canvas,
by Sherry Simone

after rain has rinsed
the silver skin of stone
& showered the brazen
breasts of trees, after the stream,
rising high, comes across
roots that have always been
unearthed. Drink, now, old forest,
while the moon pokes
its luminescent head
through the clouds' thick curtains
& with a wave of its wand,
turns all things blue.
Here, sip the hue of mystery's deep
brew, let it burn
like whiskey in your throat
as you hear the owl's dis-
embodied shout,
the distant sun's complaint
of camouflage. Let your long tongues
lap up solace, recall
the seeds that once shook
in winter's fierce wind,
then landed in this place,
squeezed between rocks
to reach the soil's strong hold.

Taste your shadows, floating
on the water, their flavor strong
& smooth as the dark
contour of dawn.

What the Stone Knows

Kids are in the barn, drinking.
They stagger out around 2 A.M.,
giddy in the cool air.
One of them trips over me,
bottle flinging from hand,
crackling on my head.

As they drive away, I hear one—
the girl—howl like a she-wolf,
her voice trailing the truck as it dips
below the hill.

  *

Red-tailed fox wanders through
just before the sun unveils
the horizon.
     Walking the dry creek bed
alone, nose to the ground,
its tongue licks my beer-
dappled face.

  *

Beneath the strangely still-visible
moon forsaking what? sleep?
a day at the beach?
(I don't really know),

garter snake slides
beneath my damp-dug
darkness. Waits.
                    The farmer drives past,
his combine humming, gravelly-voiced,
rattling the brown shards of glass
against a hornet's bulbous belly.

A blade of grass quivers
in sync with the snake's slow pulse.

    *

Silver cloud covers noon's
bright eyes. I look up.
See myself.

    *

Soon to be submerged again.
The creek sings in my ear, softly first,
a low note, or two, working
its way to full-on strum.

    *

Dusk doesn't fall,
doesn't trickle like water
or creep in like a cat.
Doesn't bottle the sun

& throw it into the sea.
Dusk lifts the light from view—
I know this first-hand—
then hides it like a key

beneath a stone.

Vessels

Vessel, mixed media on canvas,
12" x 24" by Mona Gazala

There are four, side by side, standing
    on plain pedestals, one & the same.

You love the dark lines of their mysterious
    hieroglyphs, the rivers of their silhouettes—

their long lean necks, pear-plump hips.
    You want to peer into all of them.

Perhaps, they carry the elements
    of your desired blessing,

fabric of your breath.
    Of course you think of Keats,

how one day *old age*
    shall this generation waste,

so you picture the urn, ashes
    of your grandmother within, settling.

You remember, too, the way you stood
    at her grave, summoning the spirit

of your childhood to stand witness
    to your grief, invoke the image

of her candy tin bejeweled
 with rainbow hues,

M & Ms mounding inside.
 You wish every vessel would fill

with such sweet potential, supply
 bliss that cannot be contained.

For you know a time always comes
 when you'll stare at a stone

engraved with a name you once spoke
 in the course of casual conversation,

name then heavy on your tongue,
 since each clay body empties

& falls, eventually, to the ground.

Sparrow

I picked up the fallen chick
like a fragile figurine, glass-
blown & pink as flesh,
toted its small breast,
downy head, broken wing

into the house where my mother
in her apron, spoon in hand,
turned from the pot of broth
boiling on the stove
to see this helpless thing

& me, carrying it,
cradling it in the hollow
of my palm like a precious word
or the prayer I spoke one summer,
asking the giver of my life to save this one.

Full Flower Moon

—for all the women at Safe Harbor House

The moon tonight smells like linen,
clean & pressed, spreading
its blue fabric over not just May's fields

but the willow by the pond,
the hens in the one-window coop,
the dog on the lawn,

poking her nose into the myrtle.
The sky tastes like a mug of tea,
warm & smooth with cream,

served at a welcoming table.
Should God suddenly speak,
the phlox would not be flummoxed

or the red-tailed fox baffled.
After all, green already
pulses through everything,

its rhythm in sync with this full
flower moon & the worm
below, writing a new word in dirt.

Would it really be so strange
if the still, small voice broke open
like a bulb beneath the earth,

then aired something sensible
as the strong stem lifting high
its lit lantern, signaling us

to join in, do what we were made to do?

Open Window One Summer Night

I lie in bed alone,
wind chimes tintinnabular,

their descant small as buttercups
sipping starlight in my yard

or chipping sparrows cheeping
in the puddle by my drive,

each sliver of sound
a tick of time

past memory of marriage,
a melodic shadow

trailing the life
I never dreamed of.

Hesperis Matronalis

Come with me, sister scientist, along the path
where honeysuckle's sweet incense
envelops everything—robins rustling in the walnut tree
& a rabbit running from the red-tailed fox
still slinking in the underbrush.

Hear bluebirds, sparrows, & cardinals
antiphonal from their pews
as the mockingbird chimes in
(you know it's him because you see
his white-tipped wings descend,
then wave the tall grass's tassels).

Feel how the vista opens
into farmland expanding all around,
become like the hay in its natural state,
borne from seeds broadcast like good news—
before the cutting, windrowing,
baling—
        breathe the loam nearby
awaiting corn's clean ascent,
the line between crops as undeniable
as the blossoms sprouting ripe
almonds on Aaron's priestly rod.

Along the edges shoot dame's rockets,
some three feet high—their petals
a commotion of white, pink, & purple.
Though you know why some people protest
their invasive splendor, you want
to walk among them now that it's afternoon.
So we do.

We discuss their other names—
damask violet, queen's gilliflower, summer lilac,
mothers of the evening—
                               & we consider their cousin,
the mustard seed. We wait for their scent
to crescendo as dusk's mauve gauze
drapes around our shoulders.

Big Basin Sagebrush

Beneath the high desert sun,
on steppes & Santa Fe trails,

sagebrush, silver-green & wide as angels' wings,
smells of muted camphor, something between rosemary

& evergreen, the foliage narrow as their needles,
though longer, & soft as any Midwest leaf—

honeysuckle, willow, ash.
Barely-yellow flowers air their small sentiments

atop the shrubs, largely unnoticed as every hiker
goes past. They don't care. They could live

a hundred years reflecting the crescent moon
lingering above them, spreading shade & water

to neighboring plants, guardians of the path,
their sole ambition to lead this unassuming life.

Yellow Springs, Ohio

I'm already against the next war, declares a bumper sticker on a green pick-up parked in front of the café where I sit behind a large window. Espresso steams in the back, aroma of roasted almonds infusing my deep breath, voice of the spigot, rasping. Outside, a silent movie. Two men holding cell phones move their mouths. One, wearing a beige fedora, sits in a Ford F-150 across the street beneath the Trail Tavern sign, flickering in the mid-afternoon heat, wrought iron fence below, donning red, white, & blue bows leftover from Independence Day. The other paces between Dino's sidewalk chalkboard touting a raspberry zinger as the *cool drink of the day* & that truck tattooed with slogans, their sentiments sizzling. *Vegetarians do it with relish. (But we wear a condiment!)* Writers from the workshop pass by & wave. Standing by a tree, a guitarist, his case propped open, strums. *Be ashamed to let it die. Save Antioch NOW.* The man in the hat steps from his truck, leash in hand, followed by a black & white Boxer, which, until then, had been concealed. Dave Chappelle, too, long bandana hanging from the back pocket of his jeans like Rapunzel's hair out her castle window, appears. Lights a cigarette. Chats with a brunette. A man sporting dreadlocks approaches; they grab hands, wrapping their wrists around each other's. A silver SUV slows, its driver doing a double-take, gawking as long as traffic allows. An orange butterfly floats by the crossroads of the Kingsyard StopShop, enters the gate of Asande Imports. *Break the Chains! Shop at Independent stores. (MALL WART.)* Another man comes through, tying the sleeves of his shirt around his waist, the red ink of a lobster stretching across his entire back, glistening in the sun. *Thou Shalt Not Covet Thy Neighbor's Country.* A fly blunders against the glass, lifting its sticky legs from time to time, trying to fly. Chappelle answers his cell, then walks to his motorcycle, slips on his helmet, pulls away. Leaving behind the green truck, still idle at the curb. *Peace,* it proclaims in bold font to anyone who'll listen, *is the answer.*

The Poet Performs in the Theatre of Cows

There is nothing better, I have decided,
than walking past cows & their calves in the pasture,
watching them watch you like spectators, like fans.
Especially after weeks of multiple rejections
that lead, inevitably, to a wretched state
of dejection. It's downright uplifting, the sight of those eyes
glued to your every move. So I wave. I say hello.
I can't help myself. I am the center
of their attention, here in this open-air theatre.

As they stare, they chew their cud. Which stirs me
to regurgitate a poem no editor seems to want to publish.
A poem I love, mind you. A poem, I'm suddenly convinced,
they'll love, too. I recite aloud every fat & juicy verse
on the stage of my rural road.
I say the words with emphasis,
not the way some poets at public readings lift
the pitch of their monotone voices at the end of each line
like they've somehow gone Scandinavian,
but that kind of thespian emphasis with suspenseful
pauses, eager enunciations. A Shakespearean
kind of performance.

Every brown eye of these four-legged, slaughter-
bound groundlings is still on me.
Some even stop their masticating, hang
their mouths wide open. Even the young ones,
who had been fidgeting in the field before I came along,
seem mesmerized. I finally have a captive
audience. When I finish, I leave them
utterly speechless.

Heartland

I am sitting in the shade
    watching my son's baseball game
as the other team's coach squeals like a monkey,
        then yells, *I want another banana!* to his players
            on the field while he stands
                atop their empty bench.
They are losing by nine runs.
    It's hot as Texas as the sun bakes
the boys' skin like dough,
        as they sweat like pepperoni.
            Our attention is, to say the least,
                divided. Sucking on lollipops,
we chat about the biology teacher
    who disappeared in April. The break-
down rumors. Then the punishments the school
        doles out like candy at a parade.
            By the handful. With apparent glee.
                We cheer on cue,
for high heat that gets a batter swinging
        & missing, for line drives
snagged, hits in the clutch.
        For my son's teammate who steals home.
            Cigarettes & popcorn smoke the Sunday
                air like ham, while the other team's
second coach walks back & forth in his dugout,
    which isn't dug out at all,
flashing his tattoos on each calf:
    on the left, coins & cards—
            ace, king, queen, jack—

     on the right, hogs wallowing in tame cliché.
Between innings, we snicker as the ump approaches
  the sideline, his muscle T-shirt baring the sharp fangs
of his tattoos, & kisses his girlfriend while she
    flashes her jewel-pierced tongue.
      A batter comes to the plate,
        & our talk turns to the missionary's story
from church this morning—
  the coups in Chile in the '70s—
how men thrust machine guns into his chest & yanked him
    from his house. How when the general heard him tell
      what he believed, the whole gospel story,
        he let him walk.

Moon When All Things Ripen

Late August moon, its full face
brilliant in the blue-soaked sky,
hovers over morning. The thick air
of summer has lost its weight,
thinned into the cool dry wind
that will soon turn the leaves
crisp, chill the trees' brave bones.
My daughter has gone to college.
I find myself standing in her room,
staring at her vacant, neatly made bed.
Why do I dust her table & dresser,
taking care to arrange whatever
she's left there—a broken
necklace, half empty bottle of lotion,
three brown buttons—
in such precise places?
Why call the dog to come,
speak in low tones as she circles
the room, snuffling every remaining
scent? When I look out the window,
I see my daughter at ten,
riding her bike for the first time alone,
up the hill to her friend's house,
less than half a mile away.
I remember how, distracted
by my son, I returned
to discern only the rider-
less Schwinn, already in that drive.
O, that absentminded moon: Star-

struck, it has forgotten the time
& lingers with the light.

Serpent Mound

Peebles, Ohio

    Great green leaf afloat on water,
    motionless in a creek
    after days of August sun—
      nearly a year after my divorce,
       I hike with my son
        in the Arc of Appalachia,
      land where the Fort
    Ancient people
    formed their mysterious mounds,
  like the serpent we will view
    from a scaffold above
      (no one walks on the shape),
       sinuous earth erected
        a thousand years ago
      by moving soil with one hand-
    woven pail after another,
   so the curves in the body
  point to each solstice
    & equinox,
      to the time for planting
       or harvest,
        & in the neck,
         triangular altar
       endures
      where sacrifices ablaze
      aimed to appease a primal god.
    What they believed
  about death & burial
is history's best guess,

   their creed unwritten
      in the stones
         they left unturned,
            their presence residual,
           plain as the grass
        someone mows
       every summer,
      lest the snake fade
    like pain, like the crater
below, meadow
    roaring open eons ago
      when an asteroid
        thundered down,
        before the stream hushed the newborn
        hollow & sycamore trees soared.

Three Questions

1.

Along the Beaver Creek,
lobelia clings to the soil,
foiling its every effort
to sneak into the stream,
which riffles over rocks below,
aerating the water that fuels
the wetland where a dragonfly
squints its blue, bulbous eyes,
spying mosquitoes mating,
then steers its body
to reach their next move.
Do you dare, while traipsing
this trail & glancing
milkweed blossoms,
to covet anything
your neighbor may have?

2.

Six months later,
& a mile away,
on a lime-dusted field,
a singular tree,
its leaves shorn
& waving in wind
somewhere south,

waits.
          Winter will bear
a crop of snow,
which will deepen
with the season
& wrap around
the stoic oak. No one
will amble near for months.
Driving by, will you
sing your praise
purely from the road's
safe distance?

3.

In between, where there is so much time,
when inspiration won't spread its wings
& raise its crimson head,

when nothing but mud dominates
the wetland, when tarnished tin
is the only color the sky can muster,

what then? Will you savor the age-old scent
of the now-&-not-yet, sense its tension
in the toppled tree, damp & fungus-festooned,

as you take each successive step?

Acknowledgments

I am grateful to the following journals, magazines, & anthologies for publishing my poetry, sometimes in different forms or under different titles, & for recognizing my work in some of their contests. Many thanks.

The 55 Project: "No Heaven"

Adanna Literary Journal: "Moon When All Things Ripen" (under the title: "Aubade"), "The Road My Daughter Drives On," & "Where were you when you realized"

ASCENT: "Following the Light"

Atlanta Review: "The Poet Performs in the Theatre of Cows"

Briar Cliff Review: "Nocturne"

Cave Wall: "What the Stone Knows"

Chaffin Journal: "Easy Prey"

Cherry Tree: "PTSD"

The Cresset: "In a parallel universe"

The Christian Century: "Blood Moon," "Compline," "Full Flower Moon," "Full Worm Moon," "Mailbox," "The Philosopher & the Poet Talk on the Last Warm Day of Fall," & "Three Questions"

Clementine Unbound: "Cooper's Hawks"

Cumberland River Review: "Molasses" & "Nest in a Winter Tree"

Dogwood: "Close Range" & "The Conversation of Wood"

Ducts.org: "Cryoseism" & "Vessels"

Flights: "Yellow Springs, Ohio"

Free Lunch: "Certainty" & "Science Lesson"

Freshwater: "There is No Violence Here"

Image Journal: "Full Thunder Moon"

Midwest Poetry Review: "Coming Close"

National Poetry Review: "Four days after Mother's Day"

New Madrid: "Comet"

New Ohio Review: "I never met a flower that yelled at me"

Nimrod: "Aftershock," "I was led to believe," & *"Loose Stone"*

Paterson Literary Review: "Barley Moon"

Poetry South: "Tear"

Prairie Schooner: "Weights & Measures"

Redheaded Stepchild: "Walking on the Roof"

River Poets Journal: "Blackberry Seeds"

Riverwind: "Reflex"

Rock & Sling: "Sparrow" & *"What If Feels Like"*

Ruminate Magazine: "Objects in Mirror Are Closer Than They Appear"

Saint Katherine Review: "Morning Prayer"

The Southern Review: "Heartland"

Terrain.org: "Once" (under the title "After Watering") & "This is the landscape left"

Valparaiso Poetry Review: "Barn Burning" & "Big Basin Sagebrush"

Verse Wisconsin: "The Problem with School"

Waccamaw: "Palm Sunday"

Whale Road Review: "Full Hunger Moon"

Windhover: "Hope" and "Full Long Nights Moon"

Writecorner Press: "Web"

"The Poet Performs in the Theatre of Cows" was published in *Every River on Earth: Writing from Appalachian Ohio*, edited by Neil Carpathios (Ohio University Press, 2015). It also appears in *From the Tower: Poetry in Honor of Conrad Balliet*, edited by Steve Broidy (Main Street Rag Publishing Company, 2016).

"Piano Lesson" was published (as "Requiem for the Liberal Arts") in *How Higher Education Feels: Commentaries on Poems That Illuminate Emotions in Learning and Teaching*, edited by Kathleen M. Quinlan, Oxford Learning Institute, University of Oxford, UK (Sense Publishers, 2016).

"This is the landscape left," "Nest in a Winter Tree," & "Following the Light" appear in *A Rustling and Waking Within: An Anthology of Ekphrastic Poetry Inspired by the Arts in Ohio*, edited by Sharon Mooney (Ohio Poetry Association, 2016).

Awards & Recognitions

"Certainty" & "The Problem with School" earned Pushcart Prize nominations in 2008 & 2010 respectively

"Science Lesson" won the Rosine Offen Memorial Award for best poem in Issue 40 (Fall 2008) of *Free Lunch*

"Comet" was a Finalist in the 2011 *River Styx* International Poetry contest

"Orb Weaver" (as "Web") won the Editors' Choice Award in *Writecorner Press*'s 2012 contest

"Aftershock," "I was led to believe," & *"Loose Stone"* placed as a Finalist in *Nimrod*'s 2013 Pablo Neruda Contest

"Cryoseism" & "Vessels" were featured as "Highlights" of Issue 31 (Summer 2013) of *Ducts.org*

"Close Range" & "The Conversation of Wood" placed as a Finalist in *Dogwood*'s 2014 poetry contest

Many thanks to fellow poets & readers along the way whose insights & guidance enabled me to revise individual poems in this collection: Don Martin, Margaret MacKinnon, Ron Offen, Maureen Fry, Myrna Stone, Cathryn Essinger, Belinda Rismiller, Lianne Spidel, & Barbara Crooker. Much appreciation goes to Conrad Balliet as well who faithfully hosts The Tower Group twice a month at his home, a group that often heard, read, & responded to my early drafts. Several people in that group also offered me helpful feedback on specific poems: Steve Broidy, Sharon Luster, Kathy Austin, Robert Paschell, Carol Stoner, & Janeal Ravnal. To my fellow Glen Workshop participants & teachers, Martha Serpas, Gregory Orr, & Robert

Cording: Thank you as well for your close reading, beneficial criticism, & inspirational instruction. As always, thank you to the Antioch Writers' Workshop for your continuing inspiration for and support of my work.

Thank you to my sister & her family, my brother & his family, & my parents, who inspired some of these poems, for their unconditional love, ongoing prayers, & constant encouragement.

Finally, thank you to my daughter Ashley, my son Alex, & his wife Abi, whose undying support for my work & blessing upon this book enabled it to come to fruition. Deepest gratitude to Alex, gifted writer in his own right & editor extraordinaire, who put in many hours, yea, weeks & weeks, of work to help me make necessary rewrites & compile this entire collection. You three are the salt of my earth. You are my beloveds.

COLLECTIONS IN THIS SERIES INCLUDE:

Six Sundays toward a Seventh by Sydney Lea
Epitaphs for the Journey by Paul Mariani
Within This Tree of Bones by Robert Siegel
Particular Scandals by Julie L. Moore
Gold by Barbara Crooker
A Word In My Mouth by Robert Cording
Say This Prayer into the Past by Paul J. Willis
Scape by Luci Shaw
Conspiracy of Light by D. S. Martin
Second Sky by Tania Runyan
Remembering Jesus by John Leax
What Cannot Be Fixed by Jill Peláez Baumgaertner
Still Working It Out by Brad Davis
The Hatching of the Heart by Margo Swiss
Collage of Seoul by Jae Newman
Twisted Shapes of Light by William Jolliff
These Intricacies by Dave Harrity
Where the Sky Opens by Laurie Klein
True, False, None of the Above by Marjorie Maddox
The Turning Aside anthology edited by D.S. Martin
Falter by Marjorie Stelmach
Phases by Mischa Willett
Second Bloom by Anya Krugovoy Silver
Adam, Eve, & the Riders of the Apocalypse anthology edited by D.S. Martin
Your Twenty-First Century Prayer Life by Nathaniel Lee Hansen
Habitation of Wonder by Abigail Carroll

www.ingramcontent.com/pod-product-compliance
Lightning Source LLC
Chambersburg PA
CBHW032231080426

42735CB00008B/804